THE OIL IN MY LAMP

DR. MONICA B. YOUNG

Table of Contents

Acknowledgement

The completion of this book would not have been possible without the expertise of my author coach Zaneta Wooden. She has been instrumental in walking me through the steps of writing and releasing my first book. She showed patience, professionalism, and wisdom to help me when I stepped on some emotional triggers while writing this book.

I would like to thank my amazing husband Rick Young for being by my side every step of the way. He has been my wingman cheering me on and encouraging me to let my voice be heard. I would like to thank my children for their support and encouraging words during challenging times.

Most of all, I would like to thank God for giving me the courage to write and publish this book. It can be risky business, but I now have the strength to raise my voice and use some of my own personal experiences to inspire and edify others.

Photo by Merritt Thomas on UnSplash

Dedication

This book is dedicated to family, friends, and those who are trying to find their voice. Through this short, easy read, this book will empower those who are struggling to fly like an eagle and live a victorious life in the face of adversity.

The Oil in My Lamp

I remember like it was yesterday even though it was twenty years ago. We lived in San Antonio, Texas, my husband was stationed in the military and we were stationed at Randolph Brooks Air Force Base. We had been invited by the pastor so we set out the night before to find the location of the church just to make sure we knew where the church was located so that we would be on time. At first, we could not find the church according to the address; and after looking around for a while, we realized the church was in a strip mall.

We were so used to the traditional church being in a building with stained glass windows and a standalone building, this was our first time being exposed to a church in a storefront. Nevertheless, we went to the service the next day. The service was quite different but we were drawn there to make it our church home.

Wednesdays were midday prayer at noon. I was not working at the time, so I started attending prayer with other members that came by on their lunch break. We had some powerful revelatory prayer sessions in that place during midday prayer. I had never been a part of prayer in that way. Don't get me wrong, I went to church and I love going to church even from a child, but my parents worked so many hours and we didn't go to service in the middle of the day, especially on a weekday. I was raised up in the Christian Methodist Episcopal Church (C.M.E.) and all I've ever known was Parkwood CME.

The Wednesday midday prayer was open to the general public; so, anyone could come in. During one of these midday prayer sessions, a lady walked in, whom I have never seen before, and never seen since that encounter. Her face is still very vivid to me; her skin was so pale white; she had bleached blonde hair and her eyes were the most piercing deep blue. They looked like two beams of blue light. She immediately came over to me and grabbed my hands.
She said,

"don't give out all your oil."

I felt a little okay, but a lot more puzzled by her words. I believed that she wanted to make sure I was taking her seriously. She gripped my hand tighter as to say, "listen and really pay attention." The lady was very adamant and it was as if she came in there on assignment to tell me:

"if people want your oil,
you send them to the oil giver."

The room was quiet and all the attention and eyes were on us.

I left midday prayer that day feeling somewhat bewildered about what had taken place. The funny thing is, I never saw that lady again. She did not ask for permission, or anything in return. When I say she didn't ask for anything, I mean a lot of people who give prophetic words or word of knowledge most often want some type of monetary offering in return. This lady did not appear the least bit interested in anything for her own gain. She did not ask permission to pray for me or if she could give me a word. It was like she was on a mission. She simply seemed pleased to deliver that message to me about the oil in my lamp. It kind of makes me sad because, I don't know after all these years if she is still living. I needed to find out how the oil applied to me and my life.

Who Would Want the Oil?

NOT ME! I can hear the sound of my granddaughter's voice when you ask her if she did something and she says emphatically, "NOT ME!"

Who would want my oil? And what is this business about the oil? When the unnamed woman went a step further and said,

"when others want your oil, you send them to the oil giver."

Then she repeated herself one last time before leaving,

"don't give out all your oil!"

I felt she couldn't possibly be talking to me! Why would anyone want anything from someone who's damaged and had wounds that went deep down into the soul like I did?

I was secretly suffering from the pain of rejection and always felt excluded and back then I still felt like the "ugly duckling" on the inside.

I grew up with low self-esteem and even while listening to her, I didn't think much of myself. While growing up, I was different and did not fit in with the norm. I was called out of my name, the b-word, and often called the black sheep. People labeled me stupid, slow, and dumb. All of these thoughts came flooding in and left me wondering what in the world was this woman talking about? Clearly, she must be mistaken! When I was growing up there were days I would sit outside, look into the sky and escape the cruel world around me. Being an introvert, there has always been a vivid creativity and dialogue going on in my mind even when other people thought, "the lights are on but nobody's home." This is not a blow to my faith, but an explanation of my personality type. Someone was always home, but I just didn't put out a welcome mat, because the chief offenders were not welcomed to come into my secret hiding place. It was also a protective way of helping me keep my sanity. I learned to ignore people when they said ridiculous things about me and to my face, as if they knew me intimately.

This event begged a couple more questions. For example: What did she mean about having oil? I didn't know I had oil. Apparently, the oil represents something special, but what did that have to do with me? This is a question I will attempt to explain in the next chapter.

The Meaning of The Oil

The "holy anointing oil" or "oil of anointing" was a vital part of ordination of the priesthood or high priest as well as articles used in the tabernacle (Exodus. 30). It was a way to dedicate them as people being set apart and holy. There are several uses for the oil and what it is used for; but for the purpose of understanding, I will look at the example of "anointing oil for the generations to come" found in Exodus 30:31.

Since I am doing all this talk about oil, I need to take time out to make it relevant. This is the type of oil that the unnamed prophet spoke to me about that day at midday prayer pertaining to not giving out all my oil. In looking back, I realize now that there were diabolical forces always at work trying to crush my spirit before I could come into the knowledge that God had set me apart; and that's why I didn't fit in with everyone else.

I believe this is what happens to many people who do not know the source of their pain. This spirit of rejection does a number on many of God's people, to make them give up before they come into the knowledge of who they are in God's eyes and in the kingdom of God. I found out by way of experience and revelation that if you are marked by God; you are also marked by the adversary to try to prevent you from entering into God's kingdom. It seems apparent that anytime you go into ministry; you are in the rejection business.

Jesus said the world rejected him, so they will also reject his disciples. It really should not come as a surprise, but we cannot get past being human and having feelings. One thing is for sure though, I can deal with it better knowing that God is with me through anything I go through, whether in this life or the life after this one.

God is the one who came up with the recipe for the anointing oil. God is the "oil giver" and you cannot "fake it till you make it." I am reminded how some family recipes are untouchable and secret to those who desire to have more of the delicious recipe. You have to have a sensitive palate to figure out the ingredients.

God's recipe to the anointing oil is found in Exodus. Just think, he shared it with humans. No matter how much people have tried to duplicate it, they cannot because they are not the originator of it. Some manufacturers try to embellish secret recipes to make it their own, but it is never like the original.

Anointing Oil Recipe

"500 shekels of liquid myrrh

Half as much (250 shekels) of fragrant cinnamon

250 shekels of fragrant calamus,

500 shekels of cassia

All according to the sanctuary shekel

A hint (1 gal. or about 3.8 liters) of olive oil

Directions: make these into a sacred anointing oil, a fragrant blend,

The work of a perfumer. It will be the sacred anointing oil.

Then use it to anoint the tent of meeting,

The ark of the covenant law,

The table and all its articles,

The lampstand and its accessories,

The altar of incense,

The altar of burnt offering and all its utensils,

And the basin with its stand.

You shall consecrate them so they will be most holy,

And whatever touches them will be holy." (Ex 30: 22-30) NIV.

I can identify a lot with the olive oil and the process it goes through for human consumption. Although obviously olive oil is only one part of the recipe, it is used widely in the New Testament as a point of contact for anointing those to be set apart in ministry.

The olive is shaken from the tree. By the way, olive trees are low to the ground, but it spreads out. At first, it does not look desirable for use because it does not stand out like tall trees, but to me, it is in the best position to demonstrate humility. The olive tree is suited for the Master's use just like humans when we humble ourselves and walk in humility.

Then the olive is crushed, ground, and then pressed. The interesting thing is that the skin must be peeled and even broken for what is inside to be made palatable for consumption.

In reflection, I think of Jesus and how he said, "This is my body, which is broken for you" (1Cor.11:24 KJV). His flesh had to be broken for our consumption.

The oil is a symbolic representation for the anointing and a work that is to be done. Jesus proclaimed what he was anointed to do, *"The Spirit of the Lord is upon me because he hath anointed me to preach the gospel to the poor; he hath sent me to heal the brokenhearted, to preach deliverance to the captives, and recovering of sight to the blind, to set at liberty them that are bruised" (Luke 4:18 KJV).*

Jesus was anointed for a purpose and to carry out a purpose like those in modern day times. God does not apply the anointing to a person to look good or for namesake, but to lift the name of Jesus and glorify God. Jesus was very specific in his call and purpose and he proclaimed whether people received his message or not. God or shall I say the "oil giver" gave Jesus the anointing and the Spirit to carry out his purpose.

Reading the Bible is good and knowing what it says, nonetheless, we also need the Holy Spirit to give us wisdom on how to execute what it says. We need the Spirit as well as the Word of God. I used to watch this cartoon called G. I. Joe, and he would always say, "Knowing is half the battle." Through some of my encounters with people, the church, and spiritual leaders, I have more revelation about not giving out all my oil like the "five wise virgins" in (Matt. 25:1-13 NIV). The five wise virgins are like us preparing for storms during hurricane season. During hurricane season, the newscasters warn us to have a "ready kit" just in case we get hit with a storm. The storm may not hit when we think, but we are ready just in case. The ten virgins are to always be in anticipation for the arrival of the bridegroom. This example came from a time when a bridegroom that was betrothed to be married would go away to prepare a place for his bride and may take up to a year or more to return. The bride may not know when, but she should be ready for her bridegroom to show up at any time. Like in Matthew 25, the five wise brides had oil in their lamps, plus extra just in case they ran out and needed more.

They were prepared like those prepared for hurricane season, but we who are spiritual are in preparation for Jesus second coming. The foolish virgins did not prepare at all, which is why they were called foolish. They knew the bridegroom (Jesus) could come at any time, yet they failed to prepare. Now I understand why I must protect my oil. God gave it to me to give it out, but not all of it. When I get depleted myself, I need to go to the source and sit under the spout of the "oil giver" to receive more oil.

Trying to give out of my reserves instead of the overflow causes me to get burned out and depleted of any oil. Like now, we do not know the time nor the hour of Jesus' second return, so I need to be in a state of readiness at all times. It occurred to me that people want the oil because they know how valuable it is. Sometimes the one that possesses value do not know their own value because they believe the lies that the world, relatives, even those who are supposed to be in the church try to impose.

Giving your all out to someone or something can cause burnout like I mentioned before. I got burned out in ministry. I found out the hard way that every good idea is not a God idea. Even if it is a God idea for someone else does not mean that it is a God idea for me. For example, doing a prayer line over the phone. At one point, I did not realize I committed to doing a few prayer lines with different groups. Prayer is always a good idea and a God idea. But I allowed myself to be all over the place, trying to do all these prayer lines to the point of being distracted from what I was supposed to be doing. As a result, I felt tired and frustrated trying to keep up with different time zones and schedules. I could have said no or really taken the time to pray about the direction God wanted me to go. What are you saying? I am saying that some of my frustration and burnout was self-inflicted. I found out that I can say no to going to a lot of conferences, events, and what I call busy work. Guess what? Just because an event or program have always been done a particular way does not mean I have to participate, especially if it is not fruitful.

Busy work does not equate to productivity! Don't get me wrong, I have not always taken my own advice, but this is the evolved person talking. I'm like Paul now when he says in (1 Cor. 10:23 NIV), *"I have the right to do anything," you say- but not everything is beneficial. "I have the right to do anything"- but not everything is constructive."* I also like the (NKJV), *"All things are lawful for me, but not all things are helpful; all things are lawful for me, but not all things edify."* I am not advocating that people should not be dependable and committed when it comes to ministry. What I am saying, since time is a valuable and precious resource, I must be mindful of what and how I am committing my time, so I do not end up in that place of burnout and frustration.

It is sad that the same principle applies even today, 20% of the people do 80% of the work. I have figured out that I cannot always be in the 20% because for me, that brings on burnout which lends itself to bitterness. Some events that I have attended have been very profound, and there have been some powerful moves of God. It has not been all bad, but I just have had to learn not to spread myself too thin. I have also had to learn to give myself time to decompress, rest, and rejuvenate after such experiences because spiritual moves can deplete energy from the natural body. I believe that is why Jesus could feel virtue leave his body at times.

The Oil Dilemma

All of this talk about oil makes me think of David and when Samuel was told by God "to put oil in his horn" and go and anoint his chosen vessel to become the new king of Israel (1 Samuel 16). "After seven of Jesse's sons passed by Samuel", none of them were named by God to be anointed. I can only imagine Samuel scratching his head because this is the house that God told him to go to and anoint one of the sons which he had already chosen. Now, God did not tell him who it was in advance. God told Samuel to go to the "house of Jesse the Bethlehemite, and I will name the son you are to anoint" (1 Sam. 16:3). When Samuel hears the word, he was supposed to pour the oil on that person. You can see the dilemma that Samuel was faced with, which I believe caused him to have an epiphany! Otherwise, he would have probably thought that he did not hear God correctly or that he missed the directive from God totally.

Samuel asked Jesse a question, *"Are all of your sons here?"* (16:11) Can you imagine that David was not even a consideration in his father's eyes?

Talk about rejection and disregard! David did not fit the bill, look right for the assignment, or one who should be anointed. He was just "the one keeping the sheep." When God told Samuel to stop crying over Saul, *"the LORD said to Samuel, do not look on his appearance or on the height of his stature, because I have rejected him; for the LORD does not see as mortals see; they look on the outward appearance, but the LORD looks at the heart"* (1 Sam. 16:7). This is an encouraging word past, present, and future.

It is hard to know how David felt about being isolated from the rest of the family because the Bible does not talk about it. But it is apparent that David was not considered as one of the sons or doing what was noteworthy to be anointed to do the LORD's work. It does not matter because the oil was still applied. *"The spirit of the LORD came upon David mightily from that day forward"* (1 Sam. 16:13). Samuel made haste anointing David and then he left town after completing his assignment of anointing the next King of Israel, and David went back to tending the sheep. He was anointed and thrown in the wilderness.

One day my husband rolled into church with his sweat clothes on from coaching football and was told that he had to give the word that night. Luckily, I brought him a bag with a washcloth and some deodorant to freshen up. That night he was "instant" because he did not know he was going to be called and people came up and gave their life to Christ. There was a young man there who was perplexed because he thought he had to wear a certain attire (like a five-piece suit or something) to be used like that. I know because he approached me after service and he mentioned it to me and wanted to know what kind of books were we studying to receive insight and wisdom. What time of day do we study? He thought there was some "rhyme and reason" to the anointing on our lives. What he did not know was that I had to study at night when the children went to bed because it was the only quiet time I had. Many times, I was asked to preach when I had a house full of kids who were full of energy, but God gave me grace every time. At that time my household consisted of my husband Rick, me, my mom, our three children, three of my sister's children, and one of my best friend's daughters that I watched while she was working. You can imagine there was not a dull moment in our home. On top of that, I had a Hyundai as a car that our family had outgrown, but I soon traded it in after it died for a hunter green suburban that I named Nelly-belle. I used my vehicle to take all those in my household and other people and their children back and forth to church.

We did not look the part, but we were sold out for Jesus. That night my husband was asked to preach the minute he crossed the threshold; he did not have on a five-piece suit or clergy attire. We just simply wore the anointing that God had applied to us. The problem in the church is that sometimes people feel they are in control of the anointing on your life and your destiny. People are always attempting to get the credit for the anointing on your life, but God will not share his glory with another (Isa. 42:8 KJV).

In the New Testament, there was a sorcerer called Simon who thought he could buy the power of the Holy Spirit that he saw manifest through the laying on of hands of the apostles (Acts 8:9:17 NRSV). There is no methodology to receiving this power and the anointing to carry it out! Though the anointing may be sought after, it is not something that can be earned! You cannot conjure it up by being loud or charismatic! The anointing comes from God, and God applies the oil to whoever he wants, period! When people try to act like they are in control of the anointing that comes from God, they stand in danger of bringing a curse upon themselves like Simon the sorcerer, who later sought prayer from these same men of God to escape such a fate. I do, however, know one key that can save people from wasting money buying all these how to books. The Spirit of God waxed strong on Jesus as he grew and the same with David. (2 Sam. 5:10 NLT). Spending time with God in worship is the way to the anointing. God pours it out on you. It's not all these repetitious prayers, how to books, or even trying someone else's armor. It is God who will cloth you with righteousness, and all the armor, and anointing you need to fulfill your purpose; but you must spend time and commune with him. A little humor, it helps to have the Holy Spirit working within you.

When the prophet was telling me not to give all of my oil away, she was saying do not give my power away. Some leaders feel they can strip you of all your power by humiliating you in public, by stripping you of titles and dressing you down in front of the congregation, but that is all they can do. God forbid if you are a critical thinker! It is as if they look for ways to try to pin you against the wall. They feel that they are the ones who have empowered you and they are the ones who can restore you. It is quite the contrary! They can strip you of a title but not the anointing. People like that are abusing their spiritual authority to try to control and manipulate others, but I leave them in the hands of God. I was taught not to retaliate against God's leaders or touch the anointed of God. I just did not figure out until later that I did not have to continue to sit under those that ruled with an "iron fist." I do not run after titles or melt when my name is called out loud because that would be giving people power over you.

The Devil's Advocate

Years Later Saul persecuted David and at times attempted to kill him. The sad thing is that David was nothing but honorable towards Saul and respected that he was *"the LORD's anointed."* I experienced something similar in this same church that I talked about in the beginning. I loved going there to church, Bible study, Sunday worship, Women's Fellowship virtually every time the doors opened; I was excited to be there. Eventually, the Pastor there became an abusive bully. Like Saul, you never knew which person you were going to get when you crossed the threshold of the church.

I wonder how many people have experienced this sort of treatment or is experiencing this Saul and David like relationship. One minute you are the LORD's anointed, and the next minute you are having fiery darts thrown at you like you are an arch enemy. Towards the end of my attendance there, I always had a knot in my stomach and felt worse when I left than I did entering through the door. One day we had an "emergency meeting" which translated into the latest church drama or character assassination. The pastor stood three families up, one of which was me and my husband, and told the rest of the leaders, which was half the church, that Satan was going to work through our three families. The pastor also said, "none of y'all are qualified to start your own church" while strutting around like a peacock in the most arrogant and condescending way. Other leaders jumped up and joined the bandwagon and started pointing their fingers and rebuking us as if we were privy to some unknown mystery. Wow! I had no clue that I was supposedly trying to start my own church because I was too busy trying to help this pastor build up the ministry we were attending, and I did it with joy!

The revelation that I now have is how sometimes church leaders can become the devil's advocate by trying to destroy you and crush you like powder before you can even fathom the things you are being accused of. One thing for sure, if someone is telling you that you are not qualified to do something that never even crossed your mind to do, you need to seek God about that very thing. I did not have any point of reference as to what I had done to earn such treatment, but there is a point of reference you may not be privy to though. When people act in this manner for no reason, it's because they can see that the "oil giver" has anointed you! I don't know why this revelation reminds me of my fifth-grade teacher, Ms. Erwin. I was the quietest person in my class and never bothered anyone. I was a model student, but Ms. Erwin acted like she hated my guts, which was a mystery to me because I never gave her any trouble. I didn't even know I was in all advanced classes; go figure. I just always did my work like I was supposed to and did quite well because I did not like getting bad grades.

One time we were assigned a writing project, it was called a term paper back then. We had to write notes on the index cards and turn them in. My mother helped me by showing me what I needed to do and I turned in my 100 note cards. It was towards the end of the year and Ms. Erwin set up a meeting with my mother and said that I had gotten an (F) on my term paper because I never turned in my note cards. I will never forget it because my mother had to take the day off work since we lived so far away, due to the fact that we were part of this busing agenda to Matthews Elementary. My mother knew that I had done them because, like I said, she helped me to make sure I was doing them right. When I told Ms. Erwin that maybe she lost them, she laughed in my face. She wanted my mother to sign a piece of paper saying that I needed to be held back in the fifth grade. Of course, my mother refused, and on top of that, Ms. Erwin had no basis because I was not failing any subject. Ms. Erwin had the nerve to tell my mother that I would never make it out of the sixth grade. You can imagine how astonished I was to hear those words at such a young age. My mother turned to me and said, "You better make a lie out of her." I was nervous when I received my report card on the last day of school because I thought Ms. Erwin still had the power to somehow hold me back. My heart was beating fast when I looked at my report card and it said that I passed the fifth grade.

The next year, I had Mrs. Gilliam (my angel) as a sixth-grade teacher who was the sweetest lady and always nice to all of her students. She seemed to have a genuine love for her students. I always made good grades and the honor roll. At that point, I knew I was in advanced classes.

I will never forget Mrs. Gilliam because she was the reason, I was able to go to the Biltmore House. That year the entire sixth grade was going to take this day trip and had to get a permission slip sign by their parents. The cost was twenty dollars. I decided not to bother because I knew my mother did not have the extra money. As time went on Mrs. Gilliam asked me if I was going because I was one of her best students and she did not want me to miss the opportunity to go. I told her that my mother said I could go but we did not have the extra money at that time. She said that the school had come up with some scholarships and if my mother signed the permission slip that I would be able to go. I was so excited and I went on that trip. It was like a dream to see that someone actually lived like that. I just day dreamed and fantasized of what it would be like if I had a house like that. I could not believe they had a swimming pool and a bowling alley inside the house. Upon our return to the school my mother was there to pick me up. I was on cloud nine for a long time.

On the last day of school, I received my report card with bells and whistles. It said passed the sixth grade! That meant I had made it out of the sixth grade to the seventh. I made a lie out of Ms. Erwin. I bolted out of my class to make a quick detour to Ms. Erwin's class to show her my report card, and how it said I made it out of the sixth grade. She said she already knew. I did not stick around because, remember; I said we lived far and if the bus left without me, I would not have a way home. I don't know what got into me that day because it felt like I had received an extra dose of courage and boldness to shoot that lie down. As I look back, the fact that she said she already knew means that she had been watching and waiting for me to fail since she had marked me with that word curse. I am extremely humbled to know that people can try, but they cannot curse who God has marked as blessed.

When your adversary is telling you what you are not, most likely you are; for example, "you're not qualified, capable, and anointed." That means they are threatened that you are qualified, capable, and anointed. I found out also, other people bragging about you or pointing out that they see the anointing on your life can be the spark for jealousy if that leader is not confident and secure about himself or herself. Other people can see greatness in you that you cannot see in yourself. If you are not careful, you can end up believing the lie. I was trying so hard to figure out what I had done wrong to have my character assassinated like that when I took great joy in lifting up that leader's arms. I was perplexed but realized that it is not that deep! It is because I was anointed by the LORD! One thing I have found to be true over the years and that is, it's okay if that leader acknowledges that you are God's chosen, but once you start to believe it for yourself, the war is on! If that leader is insecure, he or she will start a campaign to humiliate you, expect you to suck it up, and go right into worship right after insulting you and openly pinning you against the wall, just in case anyone else get any ideas.

I should not have been surprised, but I was blindsided by the spiritual abuse. Just in case anyone who is reading this book has encountered the same or similar opposition, spiritual abuse, or have church hurts, do not let it be the end or your relationship with God or the Church. Jesus suffered the same plight under religious leaders. Religious leaders of Jesus' time accused him of having a devil and being demon possessed because he was speaking truth and revelation that they had never tapped into. I imagine they were even more enraged because they were not the one who had the attention of the people. Jesus had the attention of the people because he had a heart for the people, and he was operating under the authority and the power of God.

The same accusations against Jesus in (John 8:48-59 NRSV) is still relevant to modern day accusations against the people of God from those whose hearts are filled with envy and strife.

"V.48 The Jews answered him, are we not right in saying that you are a Samaritan and have a demon?"
v.49 Jesus answered, "I do not have a demon; but I honor my Father, and you dishonor me. v. 50 Yet I do not seek my own glory; there is one who seeks it and his is the judge. v.51 Very truly, I tell you whoever keeps my word will never see death." v.52 The Jews

said to him, "Now we know that you have a demon. Abraham died, and so did the prophets; yet you say, 'whoever keeps my word will never taste death.' v.53 Are you greater than our father Abraham, who died? The prophets also died. Who do you claim to be?" v.54 Jesus answered, "If I glorify myself, my glory is nothing. It is my Father who glorifies me, he of whom you say, 'He is our God,' v.55 though you do not know him. But I know him; if I would say that I do not know him, I would be a liar like you. But I do know him and I keep his word. v. 56 Your ancestors Abraham rejoiced that he would see my day; he saw it and was glad." v.57 Then the Jews said to him, "You are not yet fifty years old, and have you seen Abraham?" v.58 Jesus said to them, "Very truly, I tell you, before Abraham was, I am." v.59 So they picked up stones to throw at him, but Jesus hid himself and went out of the temple."

In taking a deeper dive into this passage, the religious leaders were mocking Jesus' birthright, calling him demon possessed, and seeking to murder him. He gave the religious leaders that were seeking his life, the slip. In other words, he was in obscurity temporarily until his appointed time. There were times when I felt that I had been forgotten because I was in a place of obscurity, but it was just simply not my time to go fully into the ministry. People all around me were successful and starting their own ministries, but it was their time! It had nothing to do with my timing! I thought, "Maybe I missed God!" Who wants to even fathom the idea that they missed God, and their timing to go into ministry to fulfill their mandate?

Another angle to look at is how people will be so quick to accuse someone else of having a demon or a different spirit if that person worships in a different way.
Sometimes people go on "witch hunts" looking for something that is not there if a new person comes into the church.

Not that long ago, Rick and I went home to Charlotte to check on our parents. During that time, I was very ill. We attended service at the local church, and it was also Communion Sunday. The pastor said to me, "God has not forgotten you and his promises to you." She laid her hands on my chest and prayed that the spirit of infirmity over my chest and breathing be broken during communion, during communion! She rebuked the spirit of infirmity, and I was able to breathe again, which was monumental because I felt like I had an elephant sitting on my chest. Afterward, I got up from the altar and looked at the monitor; it said, "My body is broken for you!" For a brief moment, I thought that I had missed my timing, only to find out that I had been in obscurity like Jesus until now. I am not a person who likes the spotlight because I am an extreme introvert. I say that because this encounter took place in the middle of the church for everyone to witness. In that moment God revealed to me that I had not missed him. I had been in obscurity because it was not yet my time for certain types of ministries. My husband said to me, "Is this a usual practice?" I said, "No, this has never happened to me, and especially during communion!" I felt so overwhelmed with God's presence in a way that I had never experienced before!

David was in obscurity and went back to tending sheep even though it was made known publicly that he had been chosen by God and anointed through God's vessel Samuel! The in between time is a sacred time of cultivation and preparation. That's why I said that it is important to stay connected and maintain a relationship with the church and God. When your due season hits, all you have to do is walk in it. My friend (Zaneta Wooden) once said to me, you have to figure out where you left all of your pieces so that you are whole and not fragmented.

When I was in the corporate world and working in management, we had to prepare for audits and inspections, which included visits to your local establishment from upper executives who I like to call the "big wigs." If you had been following proper protocol and doing things the right way, you did not have to worry and scurry around like a "chicken with its neck cut off" to make things right. But if you were working with integrity the entire time, that eliminated undue stress and anxiety because then you only needed to tweak some things instead of starting from scratch. I liken this analogy with a spiritual application. If you have faith, and continue to work in the vineyard, while you are in your proverbial "waiting room," you will not have to worry about not being prepared when your due season manifest!

I figured out that all of the spiritual battle wounds I have incurred while working in the body of Christ, has prepared me even more for my destiny which is in front of me. Of course, I have learned not to do certain things, but it's not my lot in life to only learn what not to do. I should have some take aways that I did learn that was positive.

Never Enough

The revelation came to me that in the ministry I was talking about; I figured out that no matter what I did, it would never be enough. That provoked a question, "Am I trying to please a person or God by continuing to stay there?" It reminds me of Habakkuk 2:13 *"Is it not the LORD of host that the people labor only to feed the flames, and the nations weary themselves for nothing."* It's like chasing something you can never apprehend. Feeding the flames means to, fuel the fire, turn up the heat, or to exacerbate a bad situation into a worse state. Knowing who is at work and the timing is key to fulfilling assignments.

The children of Israel were in exile, but it was God that sent them there because of their disobedience. I'm not saying that every hold up is because of disobedience, but I am saying that sometimes it is God and not the devil that is either pulling you into a place or pushing you out of a place. Nature gives us an indication when seasons are about to change by leaves changing colors, sounds in the air, weather, etc. You get the idea. It may not be the season or timing to leave a place, but it could very well also be that you have overstayed your time in a place. It is best not to try to please people because it may be hard to leave a place or person. I heard my spiritual father once say, "when you overstay all types of bizarre things will happen." Trying to please someone who is never satisfied is just like the verse of scripture that I just mentioned; you end up making yourself weary for nothing and burning yourself out. Another ministry comes to mind when I think about when we lived in Virginia and then moved to Maryland. My husband and I were looking for a church home where in-depth teaching was taking place. I was not looking for a place that was driven by emotionalism, church tradition, and numbers. I was looking for teaching, training, and real spiritual food. We thought we had found that place in Maryland and joined the church. We were renting a townhouse, and the owners wanted to sell, so we had to find a new place to live. We decided to move closer to the ministry up in Maryland because, at that time, it was about an hour away. We were totally unaware that being in this ministry was going to be like the 1999 film "Fight Club." Pretty soon, every time we showed up, there was a new set of rules. The pastor took turns on the leadership dishing out surprise attacks, uppercuts, and TKOs. It was not a thing of if the pastor was going to pin the leaders against the wall, it was a matter of when. It was clever really. Give up your power to one of the leaders and once that leader started to feel empowered, work at dismantling the leader; start with stripping them of dignity, humiliating them publicly, and introducing new scare tactics. Since none of this worked with me or my husband because we did not care about titles or prestige, it forced the pastor to come up with another tactic. At one point, I began to believe that mental illness was involved, like split personalities, because it was like dealing with two different people at times. After watching "Fight Club" I believe that is exactly what was going on. I have to admit I looked at the movie to see if this comparison was relevant and it felt almost identical to what was going on in this church.

The bait with my family is telling me and my husband that we had the "greater seed" like with Mary and Elisabeth. We did not jump for joy or get excited. I was not looking to be great or make some great name for myself. I should have had some sort of clue that it was "more than meets the eye" when I was asked, "Why are you and your husband so humble?" The dialogue went something like, "If I tell you you're being elevated, ordained, or given a compliment your response is, ok." It was a tactic to see if I had some underlying motive for not caring about hype. The truth of the matter is that I am an introvert who will avoid crowds or the spotlight if possible and take comfort in working behind the scenes. I do not like attention because it always makes me feel slightly uncomfortable. There is a danger in trying to be great. Instead of glorifying God. That road leads to pride and destruction.

This pastor was full of game tactics, used inappropriate sex analogies that were embarrassing, and always tried to present some mysterious revelation that was filled with demonic activity, which was often imposed on the leaders. Like I said, there were many attempts to try to break me down, but one holiday occasion stands out in particular. It was New Year's Eve and our family had driven home to Charlotte to see our family, but we planned to return to participate in our "Watch Night Service." We were really excited and wanted to be there. While in Charlotte, my husband and I decided to go to the movies since it had been a while. I was driving up Dale Earnhardt Speedway near the racetrack. Suddenly, the truck started making a funny noise it sounded like pieces were falling then our truck stopped in the middle lane and one of the tires went flat. We found out that the brakes had come apart, fallen out, punctured the tire, causing it to go flat and somehow, the truck stopped in the middle of the road. This was perplexing because we just had brand new brakes installed by the dealership in Maryland. Come to find out, the mechanic had left an old part in instead of using all the new pieces, so the brakes came apart. It feels like there is a spiritual analogy in that. The dealership in Charlotte communicated with the dealership in Maryland after investigating to see what caused this issue. I am glad to say the dealership in Maryland paid for everything, including our rental car and gave a credit for future work. I was a little skeptical about having them do any future work since their lack of integrity created this problem in the first place.

We headed back to Maryland in our rental because we had to leave the Tahoe with the dealership to order the parts and install new brakes. We did not want to miss the "Watch Night Service" at our church, so we came straight in off the road to the church. When it was my turn to get up and speak, I told the congregation what happened and how we were in danger but had divine protection. I don't know why we were expecting some empathy, which was not unreasonable to expect.   However, the tide shifted, and we became the object of persecution, even though we were the ones who had been in danger. I mean, we knew that this was a divine intervention because we were in the middle of a busy freeway with no brakes, a punctured tire, and the truck that weighs a couple of tons comes to a screeching halt! The next day, I called the pastor, not realizing I was setting myself up to be pinned against the wall. I was told that they had been battling against the "Amalekite spirit" and I was not "qualified" to fight that spirit. Well, there it was! Finally, the pastor was being used as the devil's advocate and found a way to tell me I wasn't "qualified", which I believe was the desire all along. Remember earlier I spoke about how when you are told that you are not qualified to do something that has not even crossed your mind. That is cause for pause to really pay attention to what is being said. My response to that was, "I wasn't expecting to have scorpions on my plate when I returned home." After the initial gut punch feeling of disbelief and the gall and nerve of the pastor because we thought showing up demonstrated how dedicated we were and plus we wanted to be a part of the service. That is the reason we still raced back to Maryland, even after all that happened. When I thought about it, I remembered that no one was qualified or capable of defeating the Amalekites and that spirit which perpetuated through generations because of Saul's disobedience to destroy them. It was God that had to come and intervene (Exodus 3). The point was not about the Amalekite spirit that Saul did not destroy, but to have room to say I was not qualified.

The pastor wanted to be able to utter these words, "You are not qualified!" These words remind me of what Satan uttered to Eve, "Has God said?"

These words cast doubt or make a person doubt themselves and wonder, "Is God the true voice that we are really hearing." There was always some form of pride that the pastor had some greater anointing because of always dealing with some demonic entity. There is power in knowing the Scripture for yourself. I began to figure out that no matter what we did, it would never be enough, and according to the pastor, none of us could ever seem to please God either.

The last straw for me was when the pastor got mad at me and my husband over something that was happening at another church with the youth group. I did not know we were responsible for that other church. I counted, and it was a solid three months that the pastor did not speak to either of us and did not want to touch us either, as if we had some other spirit. I figured out then that pastor was no longer my leader, and it was time for me to make a change. Remember, I said I am an introvert so I am ok if I don't talk. I knew that this was different because I began to feel that we can play the "silent game" till the cows come home because I will win this one! It felt like war and I had my war clothes on. I also knew at the same time that this type of warfare is dangerous because it can make you cold, which I cannot afford to be as a Christian and a leader in the Body of Christ.

If someone who is supposed to be your pastor can go on and not speak to you for three months over something so menial, you have to ask yourself, "Is that person really your leader?" On top of that try to treat you as if you have some sort of other spirit when they are the one who have a spirit of bitterness. There were several indicators and signs to let my family know that no matter what we did, it would never be enough. I really believe the real problem is that were not needy and easy to manipulate and control with mind games that was infuriating to the pastor.

God Gave Clearance

The thoughts in this chapter are a collection of recollections of my relationship with the church in Maryland. I had grown weary of belonging to what I call the "Fight Club." I was praying for a way out and a change, and finally it came. I had this thought that God would speak to my husband, or give us a sign that it was time for us to go. God did speak to my husband to release me and I felt released. I left the right way, since the pastor was not speaking to me, I wrote a letter saying that I was leaving as a member, turned in my credentials with the church keys, and left. *"God is no respecter of persons"* (Acts 10:34). People will succeed in trying to minimize your gifts, callings, and anointings if you are not aware of how God sees you.

The real last straw was the day we planned to have a cookout to celebrate my daughter Janae's graduation from North Point High School. We invited friends, family, and church members. It was the same day as intercessory prayer for the church in Maryland. We had a great number show up. The chief elder attended, and I said to her that I had forgotten to send out some correspondence for the church and she abruptly cut me off and said, "We are not going to discuss any of that so we can stay focused on celebrating your daughter's day." She must have noticed the confused look on my face and then she said, "Oh, what were you going to say?" I guess she thought I had read the email sent to me that day by the pastor telling me and my husband were basically fired from any duties we had in the church and running everything through the chief elder. It occurred to me later that she must have thought I was talking about that email, but I did not even know I had the email at that point. It was not until the next day, when I was sitting at my computer reading through my emails, that I discovered the firing notice. I replied simply, "No Worries, we will comply." What she did not know was that I did not care anyway because I was sick and tired of the games and was happy to turn everything over. It was like the pastor used the timing of my daughter's graduation cookout to retaliate against us. I'll tell you what did make me mad is how the secular world will treat you better than that. They will at least notify you by a written documentation, sit down and explain it to make sure you understand, and come up with a game plan to change things as a corrective action. In most cases, there are levels, like three write ups and a final notice before being fired. That wickedness did not work because I did not even read the email until the next day. The pastor was always attempting to sabotage someone feeling good if they had a special event or date going on in their life that was not directly related to the church. That is the spirit of domination, control, and manipulation, which is a form of witchcraft. When I look back It was always like that, like there was some competition between loyalties.

Anyway, back to me leaving the church. Like I said, my husband released me even though he did not feel released at that time. The pastor was shocked and wanted to set up a meeting with me, but I let my husband handle that since I was no longer a member and we had not had a conversation for three months. The funny thing is that the pastor could not find the email and said it did not mean we were fired from our positions. I really did not care about the position, but it did bother me how it was done through an email. I have been in management for quite some time and we treated the employees better than that. When hiring an employee and sending them through so much training for them to do their job is an investment. The investment is preserved by teaching, training, and communication. If everyone is fired every time they make a mistake, there would not be any workers left to run the business or run it correctly. You owe it to them to let them know what they are doing wrong. Otherwise, you are setting them up for failure. I feel the same analogy applies to the church.

Parishioners and the people in the pews are supposed to be fully equipped to do the work of the ministry through teaching, training, and empowering. I truly believe that some church leaders do not know how to pour into their parishioners. I also feel that some leaders cannot handle having more than a few people to lead. Once the membership grows, they start bullying and acting out. Also, some leaders do not want their parishioners to succeed if those leaders are insecure. What is sad is that parishioners usually trust their leaders to be godly, spiritual, and at minimum care about them. It is a nasty form of treachery when those leaders really cannot stand their parishioners, and at every turn and opportunity look to tear them down.

I believe I stayed in that ministry for so long because I used to say, "I am loyal to a fault." God said that I needed to show that type of loyalty towards him. After all, God knows my personality, character traits, and character flaws, but I do not have to sit under someone who is a spiritual bully. I do not use that saying anymore. I began to ask myself, why would I volunteer to continue to go somewhere that I keep getting beat down and I feel worse when I leave? The answer is, I do not have to. For one, God is not limited to one location in the land. That type of thinking entices people to worship the place instead of the creator. My anointing was not valued, so it was relocated.

The Bible says that God has made a way for our own deliverance. It says in (1 Cor. 10:13 AMP):

"No temptation [regardless of its source] has overtaken or enticed you that is not common to human experience [nor is any temptation unusual or

beyond human resistance]; but God is faithful [to His word - He is compassionate and trustworthy], and He will not let you be tempted beyond your ability [to resist], but along with the temptation He [has in the past and is now and] will [always] provide the way out as well, so that you will be able to endure it [without yielding, and will overcome temptation with joy].

The test was to tempt me to revert to the old Monica and how I used to do battle. The old me had unforgiveness, anger, and yes, even hatred in my heart. These are hidden iniquities that cuts you off from God. I had a way of escape through the blood of Jesus, who paid it all for me to be forgiven of my sins, especially hidden iniquity, like the ones I mentioned. I did not have to conform to those behaviors because I could leave and still be blessed. My salvation is not based on a church building, church dogma, or where I decide to participate in worship service. It is the other way around. I still love going to church and participating in worship service, and even serving people because of my salvation and my servant's heart.

There are so many situations that come to mind while visiting these places from the past. I do not even know how I have gotten involved with so many places that did not know how to pour into the leadership that were ready and willing to serve. I can see the names and faces so clearly, but that is not what is important. The situations and crises that still hold some in bondage today are the real issues at hand and helping others identify and escape forms of "spiritual slavery".

The simple solution is that I have Christ in my heart and "there is no condemnation to those who are in Christ Jesus (Rom. 8:1 KJV)." Basically, I can leave! I do not have to fuss, fight, or make a scene. I can leave the right way, quietly and peacefully. I had to remember that the one who allowed you to take the test has already endured the cross for you and will give you strength not to go beyond your breaking points. When I think about it, some of these church narratives are created because leaders get puffed up in pride and do not know how to treat people. I have been transformed and have the power to walk away from situations that threaten my salvation. What I mean by that is, I do not have to yield to the provocation in a way that causes me to operate in sin. Sometimes you must leave everything behind and start over. God gave me the grace to be cultivated in a new place and space. That is what I mean by "God gave clearance." God has already given me a way of escape from bondage, sin, and even when I am proved to wrath. Besides, I do not have the energy for drama, games, and fruitless productivity.

Letting My Oil Sit

After leaving Maryland, I was weary and just felt worn out by the "Saints of the Most High."
I felt as though I had gone into a cave like Elijah, which had become a place of solitude. I did not feel much like going to church because I was tired of leaving church feeling worse than when I entered through the threshold of the doors. There is a difference between solitude and isolation, though. I did not realize that I had moved into isolation, where I was in this spiritual bubble, and it was just me and God. So, everything I had within me was just sitting there and becoming stagnant. I was content because you remember I said I was an introvert and therefore I do not have to talk to people. That's what triggered in me when dealing with the spiritual abuse in Maryland because the leader was not speaking to me or my husband and acted like we had some other spirit that was different from the Holy Spirit. That backfired because I have this saying, "We don't have to talk" and I fully mean that. I know the church folk will jump all over that with a scripture attack, but I am just being transparent about my personality. One thing about a

person that is Holy Spirit filled, the Spirit will speak at some point! Trust me, the Spirit spoke and said, that's your weapon. I did not have a voice growing up because it was silenced.

One day I was washing dishes and looking out my kitchen window, which I love to do, and the Holy Spirit said, "Silence is your weapon." I pondered this long and hard and had to admit to the truth that the Spirit of Truth called me out. I came to the conclusion that yes; I can play the silent game 'til the cows come home. Even if a person was speaking to me, I could ignore them as if they were a statue and not speaking at all. I will confess that it takes me a long time to get to this point, but once I move on, I move on without looking back. It just takes me awhile to get to that point because I do still have the characteristic of loyalty but not to a fault. I now reserve that type of loyalty to God.

Like I said, in this new place, I basically ran recon to check out the spiritual atmosphere. It was during the time where they had some sort of women's conference. They had a guest speaker who was also a prophet, (Pastor M). She had this crazy, wild anointing that reminded me of Samuel. I don't like being handled in a rough way, but she ran past me and my husband and stopped and backed up. She was kind of rough like Smith Wigglesworth, but she must have felt in the spirit that I don't like that type of ministry. She ministered to my husband, and she went into the inner corridors of his heart and spoke into his life. I already had an attitude and did not want to hear another word of prophecy. She said, "I'll deal with you tomorrow." I said in my mind, yeah right, by tomorrow she will have forgotten so I don't have to worry about her." Well, of course, those famous last words always get you into trouble and come back around to make you have egg on your face. She ministered so deep that me and my husband were in the middle of the church, and we wept in deep mourning. I will never forget it because it was a women's conference but my husband and I received a deliverance at that moment. He cried profusely on the good Deacon's shoulder, and I followed with my own battle cry of mourning and releasing the pain of all that church hurt in that setting. We both released the hurt, pain, and deep sorrow in that moment. God knew we were at our breaking point, and the "way of escape" came through the release of deep grief of pain and loss. I never thought it was possible for me and my husband to lament so deeply and so publicly. We felt we had lost so much; time, relationships, spirituality, part of ourselves, and the anointing. Only God can heal and seal at the same time. God is the only one who can redeem the time of what you have lost or what you thought you have lost.

Becoming Comfortable in the Cave

The thing about living in solitude or retreating too long is that it can become a place of comfort. It became comfortable for me to stay in the "proverbial cave" because then life would not be as hard. At least that's what I thought in my mind. I loved the cave because I did not have to answer to anyone or anything. Since no one knew in my new place anything about me it was easy to stay in the cave because life and the terrain outside of the cave is treacherous. There are back-biters, liars, assassinators of your character, spiritual abusers, lack of integrity, and so on and so forth. That is the image that got painted into my mind after moving into isolation. This is where the adversary of your soul wants you, so you will not connect with other people.

I thought that if people don't know your calling, there will not be a demand on your anointing. This is where I developed the saying, "The devil knows where he wants you to stay, but God knows where he wants you to go (Monica Young)."

There is always someone who can see in the Spirit! Needless to say, in my new place of worship, I went in at ease because no one knew me or any anything about me period. As a matter of fact, when I filled out my membership form where I was joining at that time, I did not put that I did too much or anything about my education. Rick forbade me to say anything about what he has done in ministry period. He was plain and simple, Brother Rick. At the end of church service, the pastor always goes to the exit doors to greet and shake hands with all that attended the service that day.

One day I tried to go through quickly and the pastor said, "We need your teaching anointing." I said without even thinking, "Oh, that's my element!" Then I realized that I let the cat out the bag that I have the teaching anointing without giving a second thought. Then I was mad at myself for speaking so quickly. It's because no matter how much I thought it was concealed, it was not hidden.

So, at that point I realized that my oil could no longer sit on the shelf, and it was required of me, not by people, but God. The rest is history. I am no longer letting my oil sit. I have been exposed so I cannot stay in the cave living in isolation. The enemy loves to get people to stay in isolation because that is the place, he can inebriate them with lies.

God Asking Me What I'm Doing There

Remember, I said this where I developed the saying, "The enemy knows where he wants you to stay, but God knows where he wants you to go." You may think that is an easy place to live, but it is a whole host of things and other people in the cave. Just ask David when he went to the cave of Adulum. He was on the run from his son's coup and landed where there were vagabonds and reprobates (1 Sam. 22). The good news is, all the people who were underdogs or in distress as well became the captain of his host and he became their leader. The cave is not meant for a permanent dwelling place, and just know you may not be alone in the cave. The cave represents a place of retreat to rest, gather strength, and get refreshed.

God asked me the question he asked Elijah, "What are you doing here?" I thought that was a silly question because, after all, I had lost my ability and gift of discernment, according to me. I had begun to question the anointing on my life. I felt like I must be off because I cannot seem to be able to get it right with discerning the leadership I was coming up under. I did not know that God was using me as a change agent and so he allowed me to see what he wanted me to see.

I do not feel that I'm alone in this line of thought. "If you can see everything up front, you probably won't do a lot of things that have actually been ordained by God to accomplish.

The Container

"No one sews a piece of unshrunk cloth on an old cloak, for the patch pulls away from the cloak, and a worse tear is made. V.17 Neither is new wine put into old wineskins; otherwise, the skins burst, and the wine is spilled, and the skins are destroyed; but new wine is put into fresh wineskins, and so both are preserved." Matthew 9: 16-17 NRSV

Initially, this passage is used to describe fasting and prayer. However; it occurred to me that the disciples were being prepared for a new type of spiritual interaction that superseded the old way of doing things. They probably had not fathomed at that time how they would have to function in the physical absence of Jesus. They were about to go through a spiritual transformation.

This passage also makes me think about the container that holds the oil or anointing, and the condition of the container. Back in the day, the container was made of animal skins sewn together to hold liquid substances like oil, water, milk, and wine.

Over time, the skin can shrink and can become hard and rigid. The new wine has air bubbles and when they expand can cause that which is rigid to burst. Basically, it must be conditioned because the elements change the composition of the animal skin. When I look at this dynamic through a spiritual lens, I see myself and others as being the container that possesses this new wine or oil.

The old mindset has become hard and rigid and so a new container must be used to possess this new wine. Paul said that "we die daily" (1 Cor. 15:31). If we are constantly dying, then we are constantly becoming new. "Therefore, if anyone is in Christ, the new creation has come; The old has gone, the new is here!" (2 Cor. 5:17 NRSV). The Holy Spirit is the new wine! We are able as the container (outwardly) to house and hold the new (inwardly). I have heard it said over and over, "Lord, enlarge my territory, increase me, expand me (Jabez prayer), but are we willing to die, to be crushed, to become new? If we don't die to the old, we won't be able to walk into the new!

We may feel like the old container that is battered, beat up, hit by the elements, worn out, and rigid, and not even suitable for use, but that just means we have the opportunity to become new again as we "die daily" to this flesh container. Every time the flesh is crucified, spiritual attributes have more room to live.

One time when my husband was deployed to the middle east, he brought me back a brass lamp container. It holds the oil that is poured into an oil lamp. He knows how I like antiques and I absolutely loved it. Even though the oil is emptied out into the lamp, some of the residue is left behind from the oil that saturates the container, so even though the container looks empty to the eye, it still possesses the oil that was poured into it. I still have that lamp today and it is still suitable for the purpose it was made for. Even though the elements have hit it and caused some wear and tear, all it needs is some TLC to be made new again.

Breaking for My Making

When I lived in Japan, I used to sit out on my back patio and pull weeds from my flower garden. It seems that while I was working in my yard trying to make it beautiful and free of weeds, trash, and debris, I would hear the voice of God so clearly. It was therapeutic! During one of these weed pulling sessions, I heard so concisely, "I want you to learn true humility." The image that I was shown was the cross. Jesus on the cross, which was the ultimate sign of humility. There is a lot to be said about God telling you to do something that you already feel you are doing. Looking at the image of the cross looks different from when Jesus suffered this nasty evil in my place. Crosses today look sterile and clean. Crosses with purple robes are displayed during Easter. They are displayed in churches with the finest gold, wood, and brass. They are displayed in stain glass windows with such brilliance.

The point is there was nothing beautiful about the cross when Christ was displayed in a humiliating way. It was bloody, marked with the suffering of his wounds. It was the ultimate injustice and victory at the same time. Christ did nothing wrong, but he was sentenced to die in the place of a barbarian. It was victorious because that is where the last enemy was conquered, which was death. But Christ had to die to defeat his and our last enemy! Is that what God was saying? I was going to have to die to learn true humility. That's exactly what God was saying to me. I had no idea at that time, but as I look back, everything around me was clean, nice, beautiful as I worked in my yard. It definitely did not look like the image of when Christ actually died on the cross.

Wait! I need to go back and tell the story of how we got to Japan. My husband was military, so that might not seem out of the ordinary. But he has given me permission to tell the story because his story impacts my story. My husband, Rick, was passed over for promotion to Major in the USAF twice and so he was going to have to get out of the military. He had actually signed the papers to start the process to get out!

This was painful for me watching him go through this unfair treatment process (his breaking process) because he is a man of God with integrity, and full of compassion for all those who served under him. He made sure to take care of everyone around him, and in fact, he made sure all those around him got promoted and they received favor. The problem was the false assumption that people would take care of him. This broke my heart watching him go through the pain of rejection and the feeling that he was not good enough. We did not know what we were going to do or what was next, but we accepted that he was going to have to get out of the military.

One day, I felt a strong sense that Rick was going to have to make a decision and it was going to be really serious and fast. I told him about this feeling that I had over the phone, and he called me the next day from his office and said, "Baby, guess what? "I was asked by my commander if I would take an assignment to Japan and we could have the weekend to talk it over and make a decision." What is more bizarre is that I had a dream about five Asian ladies in flight suits on the runway where planes landed a year prior. I was like, yeah right! How are we going to an Asian country when our white Hyundai that my parents had bought me when I was in college was dead and waiting for the dealership to pick up because we had traded it in for the hunter green Suburban that I had named Nelly Belle. When I take a walk down memory lane, that Suburban became like a transport van to take my family and others to and from church. What I am simply saying is that not all of God's plans make sense to the natural mind. We had no money, transportation, and we were due to depart from the military with no other plans for our future, but God knew the plans! God had showed up at the last hour concerning Rick departing the military and us not having to get out. We had considered relocating and moving back home to Charlotte, where we would have the support system of our family.

The place where we were, did not appreciate the anointing; in fact, that is the first place where the pastor spoke that word curse over us that Satan was going to work through us and none of us were qualified to start our own ministry. The thing is, that pastor was actually the conduit of Satan at that time. The reason that I say "at that time" is because people can change. I don't know if that is the case, but I am speaking of my experience at that time. The interesting thing is that all of the so-called people that were "not qualified" are all doing well in their own ministries. This is like when Balaam was a prophet that was pimped for money to speak a curse over Israel, *"God said to Balaam, Do Not go with them. You must not speak a curse on those people, because they are blessed." (Num. 22:12)."*

You cannot curse what God has blessed. Balaam was hired by King Balak, son of Zippor, to go and speak a curse over Israel. The revelation is that the adversary cannot automatically curse you if you have been blessed by God. In fact, you are the stopping force in your life. I have found out that the adversary may oppose you, but cannot stop you if you are obedient to follow God's instructions and have been blessed by God.

God began to minister to me through the Holy Spirit by saying, "I want you broken." Now back to my thought, if you think you are already operating in what God says, you need to learn, "What is God really saying?" What God was saying to me is that I want to stretch you and expand your capacity to walk in love. This was not the type of breaking where people try to do to a person to break their spirit and cause harm. It was God saying, "I want your will broken; so that my will and Spirit can flow through you at a greater capacity." God was about to pour more oil into me and I needed to have the capacity to hold it so that nothing would be wasted. Those old skins (the container) were full and had been stretched to capacity. I needed room to fulfill God's mandate on my life. I have heard this song called "I'm Available to You" by Milton Brunson and the Thompson Community Singers. Some of the lyrics say:

"Lord, I'm available to you
My storage is empty
And I am available to you
Use me Lord!"

One day when I was pulling weeds in my flower garden, I heard the words, "I want you broken." It was a normal voice, and I was trying to make sense of it. I was taught growing up to be strong, no matter if I felt like breaking. It was my protective mechanism for pain. It was ingrained in me not to show emotion and show a tough front. There is a danger to being so tough, to the point of becoming numb. It's like being anesthetized with anesthesia. I thought about how once the anesthesia administers the chemical in the body to put you to sleep, you lose full control of what happens to you. You are basically rendered powerless of changing your mind or making any decisions. You just wake up in good faith that what you had surgery for was fixed. You are not even allowed to make any major decisions right after because of the mind-altering effect the drug had on you. You cannot control what parts of life to be numb to once you enter into the not caring state of mind. Pretty soon, you can become numb to everything. But God would not allow me to be cold in that way.

God allowed for the Holy Spirit to come into my heart and make "my stony heart into a heart of flesh" (Ez. 36:26 NIV). It was hard for me to accept as a Christian that I had the ability to become numb, cold, or hard of heart because I knew that those characteristics did not align with the characteristics of Christ.

I needed to be broken! This breaking is not like when humans and diabolical forces try to break your spirit and depress you, so you won't move forward in your life. This was a clarion call from God to break me so the metaphorical dam would break, and the Spirit of God could flow freely. I did not know what all of that meant at first, but I began to understand that the anointing oil of God (gifts, anointing, ability, power, Holy Spirit) needed to be able to flow. Any root of bitterness and unforgiveness needed to be destroyed. Those characteristics are evil and hidden iniquity of the heart that I needed to be cleansed of in order to walk in liberty.

The thing about roots is that if left in the ground, whatever you are trying to get rid of still has the power to grow. I know because one time I had a tree and had the lawn guy cut it down three times. He even dug up the roots. The tree grew back. The reason the tree grew back is because some roots were still left in the ground, even though we could not see them with the naked eye. I believe these hidden sins are more dangerous because they destroy from the inside out without trace evidence of what is taking place. It is easy to see the outward symptoms of certain sins, but some roots can still be tucked away down in the corridors of your heart.

I believe that is why David appealed to God's goodness to expose those hidden things that he did not even see were at work within himself when he said, *"Create in me a clean heart, O God, and put a new and right spirit within me. V.11 Do not cast me away from your presence and do not take your holy spirit from me"* (Ps. 51:10-11).

Having bitterness and unforgiveness are hidden sins of the heart and can keep you from being in right standing with God. Exposure of those things that are like fugitives hiding away in the deep recesses of your heart and mind that can create a breach between you and God. The goodness of God allows for those microscopic roots to be exposed so they can be destroyed. I didn't have this revelation at first, but think about it.

Cancer cells can be so microscopic and undetectable, so it takes a specialist and special equipment that can detect those sneaky little cells. Once detected, every effort is made to get rid of those cells because they multiply and start destroying the rest of the body. It is hard to admit that you are capable of harboring such things down in your heart. But it's good, on the other hand, to find out they are there so you can repent and be cleansed. Do you know that in a short time that tree had grown up almost half as tall as the other trees? We thought we had gotten rid of that tree until we saw it started to grow again. It was as if stirring the ground activated the roots to come together and grow at an even faster rate. Some things, whether it is trauma, unforgiveness, hate, pain, etc., takes the activation of the Holy Spirit to expose.

Everything that God put in me needed to be able to flow through me. That is what the song that I mentioned "I am Available" means. There is a perpetual emptying out to make room for what God is doing in the present. I had to learn the hard way that only giving or ministering from your reserves will, at some point, deplete you. Speaking from a spiritual perspective, this creates an opportunity for burnout! I needed to empty out old baggage and make room for new, the overflow!

When I was growing up, every time the season changed my mom would make us go through our clothes and get rid of old stuff, or clothes we had outgrown in order to make room for new clothes. I can say that there were some pieces that I wanted to hold on to because they were favorites because I felt confident, they looked good on me, but I had outgrown them so my mother would make us get rid of them anyway. Since we were constantly growing, there was a constant demand for new clothes. If we had not gotten rid of anything, we would not have had room for the new. This old container needed to be prepared to become new for the new wine (Holy Spirit) to flow through.

Conclusion

As time went on, I began to get angry at the cliché, "Well, you learned what not to do." Even though this is true, it is not the only thing that God wanted me to learn. As I have stated before, learning what not to do is not my lot in life. I believe that God is looking for models of "what to do!" It is my firm belief that God is looking for those to showcase what it looks like to stand firm in the face of "the good, the bad, and the ugly." The olive has to go through being shaken, crushed, ground, and pressed in order for the oil to come forth. This may look like a replica of what people of God have had to go through, including myself, but God gets the glory. Once the oil comes forth, it is precious and priceless. I can see how the process was necessary so I will know how to navigate in the Spirit and the Kingdom of God. People of God don't have to be jealous of each other because there is so much work to bring in the harvest, plenty enough for everyone, and then some.

Don't get me wrong. There were times during my journey that I didn't know if I was going to make it and I felt like giving up. I went through times of depression feeling like I had missed God and God's timing. I went through times of self-condemnation and self-hatred. The self-hatred or loathing stemmed from growing up with low self-esteem. It was hard for me to accept at first that I had participated in hating and loathing myself, but I found out that is exactly what I had been doing all those years when I did not think I had much to offer anyone. Taking counseling classes really helped me do some of the much-needed work on myself to help with the healing process. Earlier on I could identity with the "grasshopper mentality" found in the Bible when the ten spies that God sent out to spy the land and they encountered giants. *"There we saw the Nephilim (the sons of Anak are part of the Nephilim); and we were like grasshoppers in our own sight, and so we were in their sight" (Num. 13:33 AMP).*

The giants in the land saw the people of God how they saw themselves. Have you ever noticed how a person may not be the most intelligent person in the room or the most beautiful, but they seem to attract people like flies? It is because they are confident and project glowing success. At one time, I thought people did not value me or my time, but in reality, I did not value me or my own time. I was training people how to treat me based on my own behavior towards myself. I suffered persecution and rejections from harsh leaders who were ruling with an "iron fist." For a while, I did not want to have anything else to do with church folk or the church period. But that is not the will of God for my life. I did play a part, and that is the hard part to own up to.

There must be an introspection that answers the questions, "what could I have done differently?" I do not have to enable people and go along with things when I know it is wrong. I can hold the leaders accountable, which I know will put you on the hot seat, but I am ok knowing God is with me.

One night I was listening to behind the cover with Zaneta and she had a guest speaker named Dina Corbin. She said, "You have to let go of things that no longer serves you." That quickened in me and let me know I was moving into a new season. I began to think about that very thing because what no longer serves me has been holding me back. The sad thing is that I have been allowing those things to rule over my life and deplete me of my God given oil unnecessarily. So, let's see, what are some of those things that I decided to let go of in order to fulfill my destiny: shrieking back, not speaking up, being loyal to a fault, shutting down, always running to the back, being like the man at the pool of Bethesda and letting everyone go in front of me, pushing everyone else's agenda, not valuing the oil in my lamp. I think there is enough said there.

My destiny is now and in front of me. I am called to teach and preach the gospel, leave the confines of the church building, go out into the community, educate, teach and train leaders in the Kingdom, snatch souls back from the adversary. The same mandate that was on Jesus is on me (Luke 4:18 NIV), *"The Spirit of the Lord is on me, because he has anointed me to proclaim the good news to the poor. He has sent me to proclaim freedom for the prisoners and recovery of sight for the blind, to set the oppressed free."*

Finally, I have my ready kit like when preparing for a storm system that comes through. Like those five wise virgins who had oil in their lamp plus extra for their journey. What I need in my spiritual ready kit for this journey called life is; love for God first, family, community, compassion, the Holy Spirit, love for Christ, a servant's heart, and a heart and love for God's people, fruit of the Spirit, etc. I am sure as we grow, we evolve adding new tools to our ready kit that prepares us for life's storm, ups and downs, peaks and valleys.

I hope this book has been a blessing to those who read it and was in need of answers and healing. Just know that it is good to assemble, but if you are in a place where you are being abused and bullied, LEAVE! RUN FOR THE DOOR! YOU DO NOT HAVE TO STAY THERE! All you have to do is find a place that is nourishing where you can grow. Find a place where the leader is secure in his or her leadership. You do not have to join the first place you visit. Some leaders will have people thinking they will be cursed and not prosper if they leave, but that is far from the truth, especially if you have Jesus in your heart.

According to the Bible, "there is no condemnation for those who are in Christ Jesus according to the law of the Spirit" (Rom 8:1). Remember, the oil that God applied within you is just as valuable and priceless as anyone else because "God is no respecter of persons" (Act 10:34).

About the Author

Dr. Young is happily married to Rick Young for 30 years. She is the mother of three children, three grandchildren, and a dog named Toro. She has had the opportunity to live in different states, and traveled the world such as Japan, South Korea, South Africa, Bahamas, and Puerto Rico to name a few.

In August of 1991 at Warner Robins, Georgia she attended a Revival where she vividly remembers, the speaker was speaking of having everything you have ever wanted but still feeling a void like there was something missing. That day she got up with a boldness and courage unlike ever before and went up to receive Christ as her Lord and personal Savior. She was born again, and since then have a burning unquenchable fire for the Lord.

One of her foundational scriptures has *been* *"Joshua 1:9 Have I not commanded you? Be Strong and courageous, do not be afraid; do not be discouraged, for the Lord your God will be with you wherever you go." NIV*

Dr. Young is the **Advance Care Planning Program Coordinator** for WakeMed Health and Hospitals (Level I Trauma Center). She completed her undergraduate at NC A & T State University, post graduate training at Fort Valley

State University with a Master of Education degree. While her husband was deployed during his military career, she felt her calling to attend seminary where she received a Doctorate in Ministry and Master of Divinity. She felt a strong inclination to do Clinical Pastoral Education (CPE). She was hired as a Chaplain Resident as she and her husband Rick, decided to relocate to North Carolina after he retired from the military. She has provided spiritual care in the clinical setting as a Chaplain for the last 8 years. Most recently has partnered with Transitions Palliative Care in a collaborative endeavor to offer spiritual care and support to patients with chronic illnesses and who are facing end-of-life decisions.

Ever since Dr. Young found her true niche, passion, and calling, she has always worked in ministry. She is an Ordained Elder, where she implemented and developed Leadership Training and Curriculum Courses, she was also, Super Intendent of Christian Education, and Youth Pastor. She has completed a host of ministerial training such as School of the Prophets (Voice of the Lord International), Basic Certification Course for Restorative Therapist (The Faith-Based Counselor Training Institute), Certificate of Completion (End of Life Clergy Course), and developed several training curriculums for New Members, Leaders, Young Adults, and Youth.

Currently, Dr. Young a member of Alpha and Omega Christian Center (Apostle Frank and Lynette Dawson), and WOWW Planning Committee for Blessed Life Christian Church (Pastors Roy & Wanda Hubert) in San Antonio TX

Dr. Young is very passionate about the Office of the Prophet and Prophetic ministry coupled with that of the Teacher, as it is her calling. Her philosophy is that a person should always remain teachable because of what it states in

Romans 11:*33 "O the depth of the riches both of the wisdom and knowledge of God! How unsearchable are His judgments, and His ways past finding out!" KJV*